Queen Elizabeth II

Mary Quattlebaum

NATIONAL GEOGRAPHIC

Washington, D.C.

To Adalyn and Olivia —M.Q.

Published by National Geographic Partners, LLC, Washington, DC 20036.

Designed by Anne LeongSon

The author and publisher gratefully acknowledge the expert content review of this book by Carolyn Harris, Ph.D., historian of European monarchies and author of *Raising Royalty: 1000 Years of Royal Parenting*, and the literacy review of this book by Mariam Jean Dreher, professor emerita of reading education, University of Maryland, College Park.

Library of Congress Cataloging-in-Publication Data

Names: Quattlebaum, Mary, author.
Title: Queen Elizabeth II / Mary Quattlebaum.
Description: Washington, D.C. : National Geographic Kids, [2023] | Series: National Geographic readers | Audience: Ages 7-9 | Audience: Grades 2-3
Identifiers: LCCN 2022023760 (print) |
  LCCN 2022023761 (ebook) |
  ISBN 9781426374401 (paperback) |
  ISBN 9781426375385 (library binding) |
  ISBN 9781426375552 (ebook other) |
  ISBN 9781426375545 (ebook)
Subjects: LCSH: Elizabeth II, Queen of Great Britain, 1926---Juvenile literature. | Queens--Great Britain--Biography--Juvenile literature. | Great Britain--History--Elizabeth II,1952---Juvenile literature.
Classification: LCC DA590 .Q33 2023 (print) | LCC DA590 (ebook) | DDC 941.085092 [B]--dc23/eng/20220525
LC record available at https://lccn.loc.gov/2022023760
LC ebook record available at https://lccn.loc.gov/2022023761

Photo Credits
AS = Adobe Stock; AL = Alamy Stock Photo; BI = Bridgeman Images; GI = Getty Images; SS = Shutterstock
Cover (Queen Elizabeth II), Pool/Tim Graham Picture Library/GI; Cover (background), Lazyllama/AL; Header (throughout), Petr Babkin/AS; Vocab words (throughout), AtlasbyAtlas Studio/SS; 1, Bettmann/GI; 3, Jack Hill/AFP/GI; 4, Keystone Press/AL; 6 (UP RT), Universal History Archive/GI; 6-7 (LO), Central Press/Hulton Archive/GI; 7 (UP), Look and Learn/Elgar Collection/BI; 8 (UP LE), UniversalImagesGroup/GI; 8 (CTR LE), Design Pics Inc/GI; 8 (LO LE), Hirz/GI; 8 (CTR LE), Bettmann/GI; 8 (CTR RT), PA Images/AL; 8 (UP RT), Tim Graham/GI; 8 (CTR RT), Chronicle/AL; 8 (LO RT), Tim Graham/GI; 9, Coprid/AS; 9 (UP LE), Ryan Pierse/GI; 9 (CTR LE), Tim Graham/GI; 9 (CTR RT), Chris Jackson/GI; 9 (UP RT), Chris Jackson/GI; 9 (CTR LE), Max Mumby/Indigo/GI; 9 (CTR CTR), Max Mumby/Indigo/GI; 9 (CTR RT), Max Mumby/Indigo/GI; 9 (LO RT), Max Mumby/Indigo/GI; 9 (LO LE), Samir Hussein/GI; 9 (CTR LE), Max Mumby/Indigo/GI; 10, Marcus Adams/SuperStock/GI; 11, ullstein bild Dtl./GI; 12, Chronicle/AL; 13 (LE), Smith Archive/AL; 13 (RT), Hulton Archive/GI; 14, Lisa Sheridan/GI; 15, Zuma Press, Inc./AL; 16, De Agostini Picture Library/GI; 17, Uncredited/AP/SS; 18 (LE), SS; 18 (RT), Central Press/GI; 19 (UP), PA Images/GI; 19 (CTR LE), Hulton Archive/GI; 19 (CTR RT), Tim Graham/GI; 19 (LO), Ink Drop/SS; 20, Douglas Miller/GI; 21, Central Press/GI; 22, J. A. Hampton/GI; 23, Everett/SS; 24, Keystone/GI; 25, Keystone/GI; 26-27, Bettmann/GI; 28, V&A Images, London/Art Resource, NY; 29 (UP), Bettmann/GI; 29-47 (LO), Keystone/GI; 30, Bettmann/GI; 31-46 (UP RT), Anwar Hussein/GI; 31 (LO LE), Anwar Hussein/GI; 32 (UP LE), The Print Collector/AL; 32 (UP RT), Lisa Sheridan/GI; 32 (LO), Max Mumby/Indigo/GI; 33 (UP), Victoria Jones - PA Images/GI; 33 (LO LE), WPA Pool/GI; 33 (LO RT), PA Images/GI; 34, Hulton Archive/GI; 35, Stefan Rousseau/GI; 36-37 (UP), Reuters/AL; 36 (LO), BI; 37 (LO), WPA Pool/GI; 38, Bettmann/GI; 39, Alastair Grant/AP/SS; 40-41 (UP RT), Daniel Leal/GI; 40 (CTR RT), New Africa/AS; 40-41 (LO), suriwgelena/AS; 41 (LO), WPA Pool/GI; 42, Dan Kitwood/GI; 43, ullstein bild - Public Address/Granger, All Rights Reserved; 44 (UP), Max Mumby/Indigo/GI; 44 (LO), Sydney Morning Herald/SuperStock/AL; 45 (UP), Chris Jackson/GI; 45 (CTR), Ian Jones/Daily Telegraph/PA Images/AL; 45 (LO), Colin McPherson/GI; 46 (CTR LE), Victoria Jones/GI; 46 (UP LE), DMM Photography Art/AS; 46 (CTR RT), Express/GI; 46 (LO LE), Leon Neal/GI; 47 (UP LE), vm/GI; 47 (CTR LE), AP Photo/Alastair Grant/PA Wire; 47 (CTR RT), Universal History Archive/GI; 47 (LO LE), chrisdorney/AS

Printed in the United States of America
23/WOR/1

Contents

Who Was Queen Elizabeth II?

Queen Elizabeth II in 1953, the year after she became queen

On February 6, 1952, 25-year-old Princess Elizabeth became Queen of the United Kingdom and several other countries, including Canada, Australia, and New Zealand.

The United Kingdom is made up of four nations.

The queen is a leader and an ambassador. She meets with the leaders of other countries. She comforts the sick in hospitals, encourages children in schools, and supports charities. Queen Elizabeth II spent her life serving the people of the United Kingdom.

But as a child, Elizabeth never expected to be queen.

Words to KNOW

UNITED KINGDOM: A country made up of four nations: England, Scotland, Wales, and Northern Ireland

AMBASSADOR: A person who represents their country

A Young Princess

Queen Elizabeth II was born as Elizabeth Alexandra Mary on April 21, 1926, in London, England. Her grandfather was King George V, which meant that she was not only a member of the British royal family, but also a princess.

At that time, girls rarely became monarchs (MON-arks). By law, boys in a royal family were always first in line to the British throne.

One-year-old Elizabeth with her mother

Elizabeth waves from the balcony of Buckingham Palace with her sister, Margaret, and her grand-parents King George V and Queen Mary in 1935.

In 2011, Elizabeth supported a change to the law that made boys first in line to the British throne. Today, the oldest child of the ruling monarch, male or female, is the heir.

That's a **FACT!**

CHRISTENING of H.R.H. PRINCESS ELIZABETH ALEXANDRA MARY.
PHOTO: CENTRAL NEWS. LTD. T.M. KING GEORGE and QUEEN MARY. T.R.H. The DUKE & DUCHESS of YORK and INFANT PRINCESS. 242.P. BEAGLES' POSTCARDS

Elizabeth with her parents and grandparents at her christening in 1926

Words to KNOW

BRITISH: Having to do with Great Britain or the United Kingdom and its people

HEIR: A person with the right to be king or queen, or to claim the throne

MONARCH: A king or queen of a country

In the royal family, the list of people who are next in line for the throne is called the line of succession.

Elizabeth's father, Prince Albert, and her mother, also named Elizabeth, were called the Duke and Duchess of York. Albert was the second son of King George V. His older brother, Prince Edward, was heir to the throne.

Line of Succession

KEY: ·············· Married ▪▪▪▪▪▪ Divorced ——— Children

① - **⑦** Order of royal family members in line for the throne

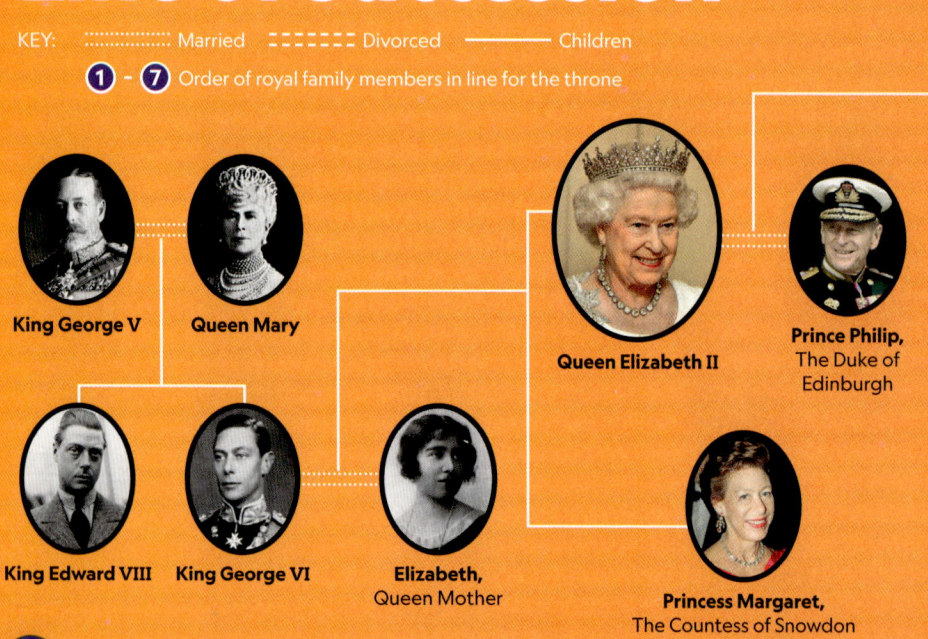

King George V

Queen Mary

Queen Elizabeth II

Prince Philip,
The Duke of Edinburgh

King Edward VIII

King George VI

Elizabeth,
Queen Mother

Princess Margaret,
The Countess of Snowdon

Roman Numerals

Many monarchs have the same names. Roman numerals are a way to tell them apart. With this type of numbering, the capital letter I = 1, V = 5, and X = 10. To make larger numbers, add letters.

II = 2
I + I = 2
1 + 1 = 2

A letter that stands for a smaller number in front of a larger one means to subtract.

IX = 9
X - I = 9
10 - 1 = 9

Roman numerals 1 through 12 on a clockface

King Charles III

Diana,
The Princess
of Wales

❶ **Prince William,**
The Prince
of Wales

Catherine,
The Princess
of Wales

Princess Anne,
The Princess Royal

Camilla,
Queen Consort

❷ **Prince George**

❸ **Princess Charlotte**

❹ **Prince Louis**

❺ **Prince Harry,**
The Duke of Sussex

Meghan,
The Duchess of Sussex

Prince Andrew,
The Duke of York

Prince Edward,
The Earl of Wessex

❻ **Archie**
Mountbatten-Windsor

❼ **Lilibet**
Mountbatten-Windsor

As children, Elizabeth and her sister, Margaret, lived in a large house in London, the British capital. Her family also spent time at their country home, called Royal Lodge.

When Elizabeth was six years old, the people of Wales gave her a great gift—a miniature cottage! It had two stories, working lights, and running water. It still stands on the grounds of Royal Lodge today.

That's a FACT!

One of Elizabeth's favorite books as a child was the horse story *Black Beauty* by Anna Sewell.

The young family enjoyed spending time with their dogs.

Elizabeth loved animals, especially horses and dogs. She rode her Shetland pony, Peggy, and played with their corgi, Dookie.

Her grandfather, the king, visited often. Once in a while, he would play with the girls. Sometimes he pretended to be a horse, and Elizabeth would lead him around by his beard.

Like most royal children, Elizabeth and Margaret didn't go to a school with other children. Instead, a governess came to their home to teach them.

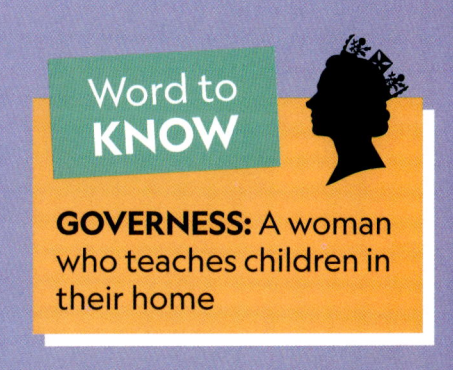

Word to KNOW

GOVERNESS: A woman who teaches children in their home

SOUVENIR OF 1936 **THE YEAR OF THE THREE KINGS**

H. M. KING GEORGE V.
Accession.. May 6, 1910.
Died.......Jan 20, 1936.

H. M. KING GEORGE VI.
Accession... Dec. 11, 1936.
Coronation Day. May 12, 1937.

H. M. KING EDWARD VIII
Accession. Jan. 20, 1936.
Abdication. Dec. 11, 1936.

There were three kings in the year 1936:
George V, who died; Edward VIII, who gave up
the crown; and George VI, Elizabeth's father.

When Elizabeth was 11 years old, life suddenly
changed for her family.

Her grandfather King George V died, and
Elizabeth's uncle became King Edward VIII.
Edward loved a woman who was divorced.
But at the time, a monarch was not allowed
to marry a divorced person. Edward chose to
marry her anyway and give up the crown.

Word to **KNOW**

CORONATION: The ceremony
in which a monarch is crowned

Buckingham Palace is the London home of the monarch and the royal family.

Elizabeth and her family wear crowns and robes at her father's coronation.

As a result, Elizabeth's father, Prince Albert, became King George VI. The family moved into Buckingham Palace in London.

Since Elizabeth did not have any brothers, she was now next in line to the throne!

That's a FACT!

When they become monarchs, many people change their names. Elizabeth's father, Prince Albert, changed his name to George VI. Elizabeth kept her name, but since there had been another queen with her name, she became Elizabeth II.

Studying Hard

Elizabeth studying in Windsor Castle in 1940

14

Elizabeth on an official visit with her parents

Preparing to become the queen was a lot of work. But Elizabeth was up for the challenge. She studied hard to prepare for her reign (RAIN). She learned about her nation's long history and its many laws. The princess was a serious girl, and she cared very much. She wanted to be a good monarch someday.

In 1939, the United Kingdom entered World War II. Germany had already invaded Poland, France, and other European countries. In the fall of 1940, German planes began bombing London.

Word to KNOW

REIGN: The period of time when a king or queen rules

War

Many bombs were dropped on London during World War II.

To escape the bombings, the king and queen sent Elizabeth and Margaret away from their home at Buckingham Palace in London. Many British children had to leave their families to live in the countryside during World War II.

Elizabeth (right) and Margaret spoke on a children's radio show from Windsor Castle on October 13, 1940.

In Her Own WORDS

"My sister ... and I feel so much for you as we know ... what it means to be away from those we love most of all."

From her countryside home at Windsor Castle, 14-year-old Elizabeth gave her first royal speech on a children's radio show. Her words brought comfort to children who had been separated from their families because of the war.

This was the first of many speeches Elizabeth would give to help her country through tough and scary times.

Queen Elizabeth II's Cool Firsts

Queen Elizabeth II was the first to do a lot of things. Did you know these firsts?

1

In 1945, during World War II, she became the first (and only) **royal British woman** to join **the military.** Her job was to drive and repair trucks.

2

She was the **youngest person** to ever be made **colonel-in-chief of the Grenadier Guards,** part of the British Army.

3

In 1953, she was the first British monarch whose **coronation** was **broadcast** on **television.**

4

In 1968, Queen Elizabeth was the first British monarch to **allow a film crew** to record the **daily lives** of the royal family.

5

In 1986, she was the first British monarch to **visit China.**

6

In 2022, Queen Elizabeth became the first British monarch to celebrate **70 years** on the **throne.**

THE QUEEN'S PLATINUM JUBILEE · 1952-2022

A Charming Prince

Elizabeth first met Prince Philip of Greece and Denmark at a royal family wedding. She saw him again when he was training to be an officer in the Royal Navy. He was smart, funny, and charming.

Philip was a lieutenant in the Royal Navy.

Elizabeth and Philip walk together after announcing their engagement.

In Her Own **WORDS**

"... He has, quite simply, been my strength and stay all these years ..."

They wrote letters to each other throughout World War II. After the war, Philip visited Elizabeth many times. They were in love. In July 1947, the royal family announced that they were engaged!

A Royal Wedding

Philip and Elizabeth were married on November 20, 1947. Her satin wedding gown was covered in pearls and crystals. The train of the dress was 15 feet long—that's the length of a canoe! Thousands of people lined the street to cheer for the happy couple. Millions of people around the world listened to the ceremony live on the radio and then watched highlights on TV later that day.

That's a FACT! The wedding cake was nine feet tall. It was cut with Philip's sword, which was a wedding gift from the king.

The couple was married in Westminster Abbey.

Royal Children

Elizabeth and Philip moved to Clarence House, their new home near Buckingham Palace. Their first son, Charles, was born in 1948. He was now second in line to the throne.

Elizabeth and Philip with Charles and Anne in 1951

The royal family at Windsor Castle in 1965

The family grew with three more children. Anne was born in 1950, Andrew in 1960, and Edward in 1964.

Elizabeth was a busy working mother and often had royal duties she needed to fulfill. But she enjoyed the times she could play with her children or tuck them into bed at night.

A New Queen

Thousands of people came to see the funeral procession for King George VI in London on February 15, 1952.

Not long after Anne was born, Elizabeth's father, King George VI, grew very sick with lung cancer. Little by little, Elizabeth began taking on some of his royal duties.

In 1952, Elizabeth and Philip set out on a royal tour. They were to visit many places, including Kenya, Australia, and New Zealand.

While they were in Kenya, King George VI died. Upon hearing the news, Elizabeth and Philip returned to England. She was now queen.

On June 2, 1953, during her coronation ceremony, Elizabeth was crowned Queen Elizabeth II. A gold crown, called St. Edward's Crown, was placed on her head. It weighed almost five pounds and had 444 jewels, including rubies, amethysts, sapphires, and garnets.

Westminster Abbey was packed with thousands of guests. Many thousands more stood in the streets hoping to get a glimpse of the queen in her golden carriage.

In Her Own WORDS

"Throughout all my life and with all my heart I shall strive to be worthy of your trust."

The queen holds the golden orb, a symbol of godly power. She also holds the scepter, a symbol of worldly power. These pieces and the crown are called the crown jewels.

After her coronation, the queen rode in a golden carriage through London.

For the first time, the ceremony could be watched live on television, and millions of people around the world tuned in. Long live the queen!

As the queen's husband, Philip was given the title of consort. Only a male monarch is given the title "king" in the United Kingdom.

Official Duties

In 1957, Queen Elizabeth became the first monarch to open a session of the Canadian Parliament.

One of the monarch's most important duties is to open Parliament. This is an event that marks the official start to the parliamentary year. She starts the session, or meeting, with a speech. Parliament is the group of leaders that writes the country's laws.

The queen met often with the prime minister. She is pictured here with Prime Minister Margaret Thatcher.

The United Kingdom has a government called a constitutional monarchy. The prime minister is the head of the government. The prime minister's job is to make sure the laws are carried out. Queen Elizabeth II was the head of state, and while she approved the laws, she could not tell the government what to do.

Former U.S. president Barack Obama and the queen in 2011

Queen Elizabeth was an ambassador for her country. She met with leaders and officials when they visited and when she traveled abroad.

31

6 COOL Facts About Queen Elizabeth II

1 Elizabeth called herself **Lilibet** as a child. It became her **nickname.**

2 The queen had **more than 30 corgis** in her lifetime.

3 Queen Elizabeth **loved raising horses** and watching them race. She **continued to ride,** even into her nineties.

4

The queen was a **movie star!** In a **film** for the opening ceremony of the 2012 Olympics, she **parachuted out of a helicopter** with **James Bond.** In another film, she **had tea** with **Paddington Bear.**

5

Serving those in need was very **important** to the queen. She supported **more than 500 charities,** including ones that **help animals!**

Windsor Castle was **damaged** during a **fire** in 1992. To help pay for repairs, Queen Elizabeth **opened Buckingham Palace for tours.**

6

A Royal Day

One of the queen's dogs sits beside her while she performs her royal duties.

The queen kept a busy schedule. She began each day with a cup of hot tea and a light breakfast. Then she received the day's news and read and signed important government papers and letters. During the day, she met with ambassadors from other countries and official visitors. The queen often worked in the evening, too, attending receptions and dinners. Once a week she met with the prime minister to discuss whatever was happening in the government.

The queen shared some of her work with her oldest son, Charles. She wanted to help him prepare to be king.

Queen Elizabeth II attends the State Opening of Parliament with her son Prince Charles in 2017.

That's a FACT!

To relax, the queen worked on crossword or jigsaw puzzles, or took walks with her dogs.

A Growing Family

The queen's family continues to grow. She loved her eight grand-children and many great-grandchildren.

Prince Charles celebrates his birthday with his sons and their families in 2018.

Queen Elizabeth II and members of the royal family gather on the balcony at Buckingham Palace in 2009.

While being a monarch was serious business, the queen also knew how to have fun. Every summer, the family got together in Scotland at Balmoral Castle. They spent time dancing, having picnics, and playing with the queen's dogs.

A favorite gathering place for the royal family is Balmoral, the royal family's castle in Scotland.

Loyal Friends

Since she was a little girl, Queen Elizabeth loved spending time with her dogs and horses.

In fact, the queen loved animals so much, she even took one of her dogs on her honeymoon! The corgi, named Susan, was a gift from her father for her 18th birthday.

Queen Elizabeth even invented a new dog breed called a dorgi. It is a cross between a corgi and a dachshund. Throughout her life, the queen had more than 30 dogs, including corgis, dorgis, and a cocker spaniel.

The queen takes a break from work to play with her dogs.

That's a **FACT!** A rule from the 1300s says that all of the whales and dolphins in the waters around the United Kingdom belong to the monarch.

The queen loved horseback riding and had many horses throughout her life. One of her favorite horses was named Sanction.

The queen rides Sanction with her daughter, Princess Anne, at Windsor Castle in England.

A Long Reign

Everyone loves a party and Queen Elizabeth's history-making reign is definitely worth celebrating! Special events called jubilees celebrate important milestones in the life of a monarch.

That's a FACT!

Queen Elizabeth had two birthday celebrations in the United Kingdom each year. At her official public birthday event, a parade called Trooping the Colour, she rode in a carriage with a horse procession. For her private family gathering, she ate her favorite dessert: chocolate cake!

1926
Born in London, England, on April 21

1933
Gets her first corgi, Dookie

1936
Father becomes king

People flood central London for the queen's birthday parade, Trooping the Colour, during the 2022 Jubilee.

The queen watches the parade from the balcony at Buckingham Palace.

In 2022, Queen Elizabeth celebrated a Platinum Jubilee, marking 70 years as queen. It is the longest a British monarch has ever been on the throne!

1945
Joins the British military during World War II

1947
Marries Prince Philip

1948
Gives birth to her heir, Charles

The reign of Queen Elizabeth II spanned seven decades. She saw great changes in her country and in the world after she became queen in 1952. The monarchy has had to adapt and evolve, and to do that, the queen helped to change some of the rules about what monarchs can and can't do.

Queen Elizabeth II and Prince Philip in 2011

1952
Becomes queen

1953
Is crowned at her coronation ceremony

1992
Windsor Castle fire

2007
Becomes oldest reigning British monarch

Queen Elizabeth II died on September 8, 2022, at age 96. Prince Charles became King Charles III. Queen Elizabeth will be remembered for her long and historic reign.

Queen Elizabeth II in 2015

In Her Own **WORDS**

"As we mark this anniversary, it gives me pleasure to renew to you the pledge I gave in 1947 that my life will always be devoted to your service."

2015
Becomes longest reigning British monarch

2022
Celebrates Platinum Jubilee—70 years on the throne

2022
Dies on September 8 at age 96

QUIZ WHIZ

How much do you know about Queen Elizabeth II? Probably a lot! Take this quiz and find out.

Answers are at the bottom of page 45.

1 How old was Elizabeth when she became queen?
A. 43
B. 25
C. 28
D. 17

2 Where did Elizabeth and Philip first meet?
A. at a horse race
B. at school
C. on a roller coaster
D. at a royal family wedding

3 Elizabeth brought a _____ on her honeymoon.
A. poodle
B. favorite toy
C. corgi
D. cat

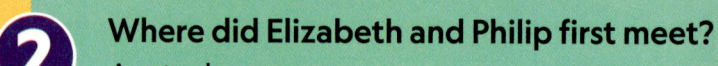

4 Queen Elizabeth's Platinum Jubilee celebrated ____ years on the throne.

A. 50
B. 3
C. 70
D. 101

5 When Elizabeth became queen, Philip became _____.

A. king
B. emperor
C. the queen's consort
D. prime minister

6 _____ makes the laws for the United Kingdom.

A. The reigning monarch
B. The prime minister
C. The president
D. Parliament

7 How many children did Elizabeth have?

A. 4
B. 0
C. 7
D. 1

GLOSSARY

AMBASSADOR: A person who represents their country

CORONATION: The ceremony in which a monarch is crowned

GOVERNESS: A woman who teaches children in their home

PARLIAMENT: The group that makes the laws for the country

PRIME MINISTER: The head of the government in a country that has a parliament

BRITISH: Having to do with Great Britain or the United Kingdom and its people

CONSORT: The husband or wife of the ruling monarch

HEIR: A person with the right to be king or queen, or to claim the throne

MONARCH: A king or queen of a country

REIGN: The period of time when a king or queen rules

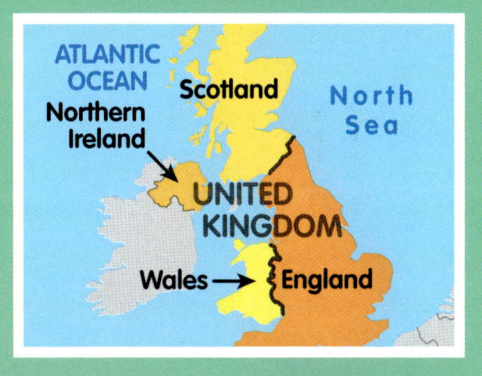

UNITED KINGDOM: A country made up of four nations: England, Scotland, Wales, and Northern Ireland

INDEX

Boldface indicates illustrations.